The McGraw·Hill Companies

Kindergarten

**Phonics • Vocabulary
Comprehension • Writing**

A McGraw·Hill/Warner Bros. Workbook

W9-CGL-658

Table of Contents

Table of Contents (continued)

Credits:
McGraw-Hill Learning Materials Editorial/Production Team
Vincent F. Douglas, B.S. and M. Ed.
Tracy R. Paulus
Jennifer P. Blashkiw

Design Studio
Mike Legendre; Creativity On Demand

Warner Bros. Worldwide Publishing Editorial/Production Team
Michael Harkavy   Charles Carney
Paula Allen   Allen Helbig
Victoria Selover

Illustrators
Cover: Renegade Animation, Inc.
Interior: Arkadia Illustration & Design—London

McGraw-Hill
Consumer Products

A Division of The McGraw-Hill Companies

Send all inquiries to:
McGraw-Hill Consumer Products
250 Old Wilson Bridge Road
Worthington, Ohio 43085

1-57768-210-6

TOP, BOTTOM

Directions: Have your child look at the pictures, then circle the picture in each row that shows *top* and put an X on the picture that shows *bottom*. **Skill:** Identifying the positions top and bottom.

3

LEFT, RIGHT

4

Directions: Have your child look at the picture, then color the ball on the *left* green, color the ball on the *right* red, then circle the characters on the *left*. **Skill:** Identifying the positions left and right.

s	 s	e	s	w
i	l	i	i	y
p	p	d	b	p
b	b	c	b	d
G	D	G	Q	G
N	N	R	N	M
Y	J	Y	P	Y
J	J	P	J	I

Directions: Have your child look at the letter in the box at the beginning of each row, then circle the two letters in each row that are the same. **Skill:** Matching capital and lowercase letters.

5

NUMBERS 1 TO 10

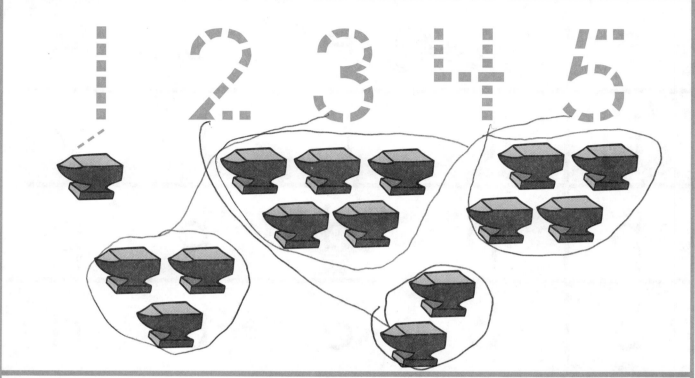

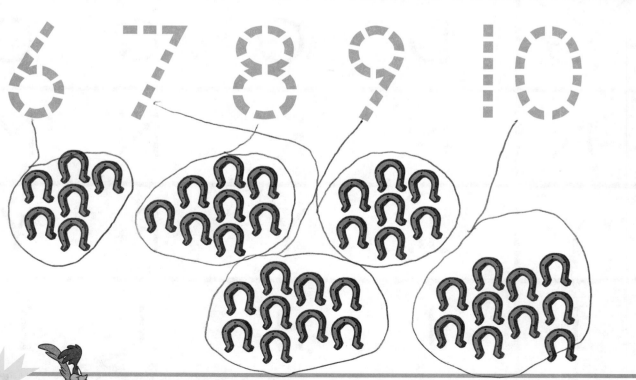

Directions: Have your child trace each number, then draw a line from the number to the set of anvils or horseshoes it represents. **Skill:** Writing the numbers 1 to 10; recognizing groups of 1 to 10.

Beginning Sound K

Directions: Have your child trace Kk at the beginning of each row. Ask your child to name the pictures, then circle those with the beginning sound k. **Skill:** Identifying the beginning sound k; writing Kk.

7

COMPREHENSION

The the

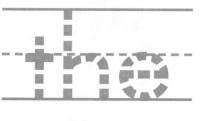 

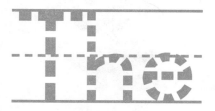 

Directions: Have your child identify the word at the top of the page, then trace and write the words and sentences. Point out the use of capital letters and periods in the sentences. **Skill:** Understanding and using vocabulary; recognizing sentence structure.

BEGINNING SOUND M

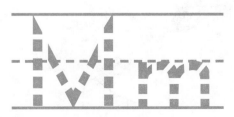  

Directions: Have your child trace Mm at the beginning of each row. Ask your child to name the pictures, then circle those with the beginning sound m. **Skill:** Identifying the beginning sound m; writing Mm.

9

COMPREHENSION

The the man

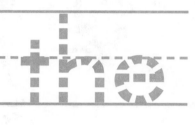  

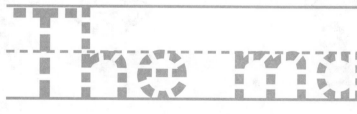 

Directions: Have your child identify the words at the top of the page, then trace and write the words and sentences. Point out the use of capital letters and periods in the sentences. **Skill:** Understanding and using vocabulary; recognizing sentence structure.

BEGINNING SOUND B

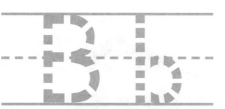

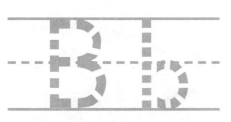

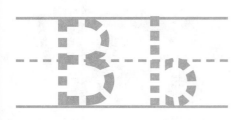

Directions: Have your child trace Bb at the beginning of each row. Ask your child to name the pictures, then circle those with the beginning sound b. **Skill:** Identifying the beginning sound b; writing Bb.

COMPREHENSION

Boys boys

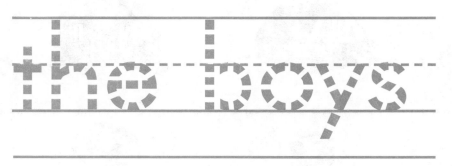

the boys

Boys

Directions: Have your child identify the word at the top of the page, then trace and write the words and sentences. Point out the use of capital letters and periods in the sentences. **Skill:** Understanding and using vocabulary; recognizing sentence structure.

NAME

Directions: Have your child identify the scenes in each box, then ask your child to number the pictures in the order in which they take place. **Skill:** Identifying a sequence of events.

VOWELS: SHORT A

   cat

Directions: Have your child trace Aa at the beginning of each row. Ask your child to say the word *cat* while listening for the short a sound. Have your child name the pictures, then circle those that have the same short a sound as the picture at the top of the page. **Skill:** Identifying the short a vowel sound; writing Aa.

COMPREHENSION

The the man

Boys boys

the boys

Boys

The man

Directions: Have your child identify the words at the top of the page, then trace and write the words and sentences. Point out the use of capital letters and periods in the sentences. **Skill:** Understanding and using vocabulary; recognizing sentence structure.

CLASSIFYING

Directions: Have your child identify the pictures, then circle those in each box that belong in the same category: the cat family, things to sit on, things to play with and things to ride. **Skill:** Identifying and classifying objects.

FIRST, MIDDLE, LAST

Directions: Have your child identify the pictures, then circle the *last* character in the first row; the *middle* character in the second row, the *first* train in the third row and the *middle* character in the fourth row.
Skill: Identifying the positions first, middle and last.

17

BEGINNING SOUND J

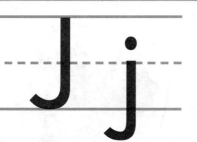  

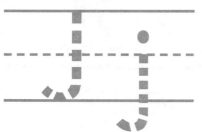  

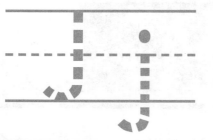  

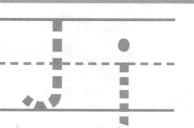  

Directions: Have your child trace Jj at the beginning of each row. Ask your child to name the pictures, then circle those with the beginning sound j. **Skill:** Identifying the beginning sound j; writing Jj.

COMPREHENSION

Jump jump

The boys jump.

Jump boys!

Directions: Have your child identify the word at the top of the page, then trace and write the words and sentences. Point out the use of capital letters, periods and exclamation points in the sentences.
Skill: Understanding and using vocabulary; recognizing sentence structure.

BEGINNING SOUND F

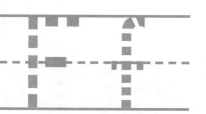  

 **2** **5**

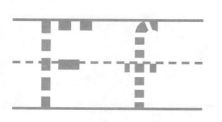  

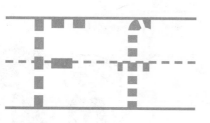  

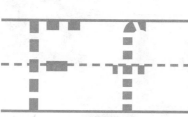 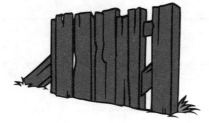 

 **20**

Directions: Have your child trace Ff at the beginning of each row. Ask your child to name the pictures, then circle those with the beginning sound f. **Skill:** Identifying the beginning sound f; writing Ff.

COMPREHENSION

fish

Boys fish.

The boys fish.

Directions: Have your child identify the word at the top of the page, then trace and write the words and sentences. Point out the use of capital letters and periods in the sentences. **Skill:** Understanding and using vocabulary; recognizing sentence structure.

21

BEGINNING SOUND G

G g

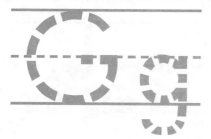  

Directions: Have your child trace Gg at the beginning of each row. Ask your child to name the pictures, then circle those with the beginning sound g. **Skill:** Identifying the beginning sound g; writing Gg.

Girls girls

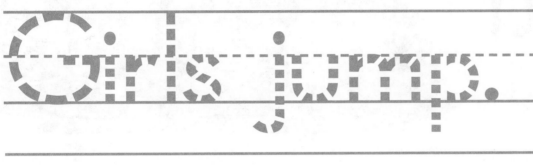

Girls jump.

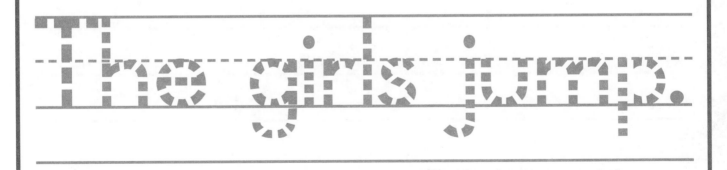

The girls jump.

Directions: Have your child identify the word at the top of the page, then trace and write the words and sentences. Point out the use of capital letters and periods in the sentences. **Skill:** Understanding and using vocabulary; recognizing sentence structure.

COMPREHENSION

and

girls and boys

Girls _____ boys jump.

24

Directions: Have your child identify the word at the top of the page, then trace and write the words and sentences. Point out the use of the capital letter and period in the sentence. **Skill:** Understanding and using vocabulary; recognizing sentence structure.

NAME

SEQUENCE

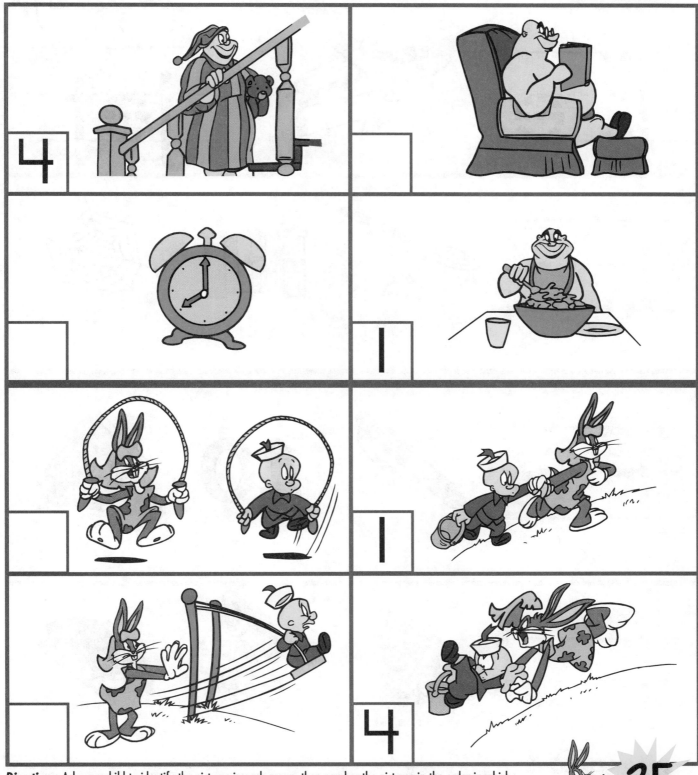

Directions: Ask your child to identify the pictures in each group, then number the pictures in the order in which they take place. **Skill:** Identifying a sequence of events.

25

VOWELS: SHORT E

E e 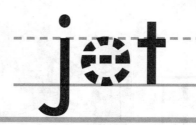 j**e**t

E e

E e 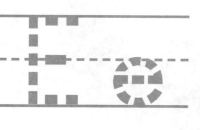  **10**

E e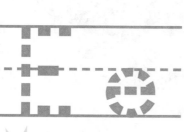

26

Directions: Have your child trace Ee at the beginning of each row. Ask your child to say the word *jet* while listening for the short e sound. Have your child name the pictures, then circle those that have the same short e sound as the picture at the top of the page. ***Skill:*** Identifying the short e vowel sound; writing Ee.

COMPREHENSION

Girls __ boys fish.
and   the

Boys and __ jump.
fish   girls

__ girls!
Boys   Jump

The girls __.
fish   jump

Directions: Have your child look at the pictures in each box, then circle the word that completes the sentence and describes the picture. **Skill:** Understanding and using vocabulary; recognizing sentence structure.

NAME _____

CLASSIFYING

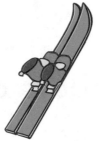

28

Directions: Have your child identify the pictures, then circle those in each box that belong in the same category: things a cowboy uses, the cat family, people who work in the city, and things that grow.
Skill: Identifying and classifying objects.

SEQUENCE

Directions: Have your child identify the scenes in each box, then ask your child to number the pictures in the order in which they take place. **Skill:** Identifying a sequence of events.

29

NAME _____

BEGINNING SOUND H

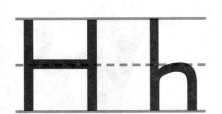  

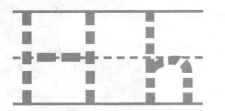  

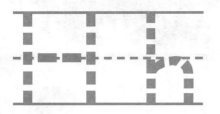  

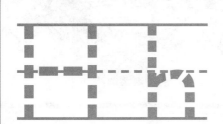  

30

Directions: Have your child trace Hh at the beginning of each row. Ask your child to name the pictures, then circle those with the beginning sound h. *Skill:* Identifying the beginning sound h; writing Hh.

BEGINNING SOUND R

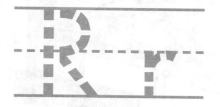  

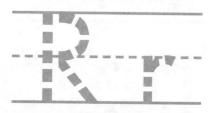  

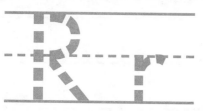  

Directions: Have your child trace Rr at the beginning of each row. Ask your child to name the pictures, then circle those with the beginning sound r. **Skill:** Identifying the beginning sound r; writing Rr.

31

Name _____

COMPREHENSION

rides

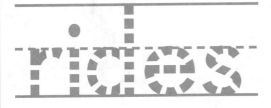

DANGER!
BRIDGE OUT

The man rides.

32

Directions: Have your child identify the word at the top of the page, then trace and write the words and sentences. Point out the use of capital letters and periods in the sentences. *Skill:* Understanding and using vocabulary; recognizing sentence structure.

BEGINNING SOUND N

Directions: Have your child trace Nn at the beginning of each row. Ask your child to name the pictures, then circle those with the beginning sound n. **Skill:** Identifying the beginning sound n; writing Nn.

33

COMPREHENSION

Now now

Jump now.

Now jump.

34

Directions: Have your child identify the word at the top of the page, then trace and write the words and sentences. Point out the use of capital letters and periods in the sentences. **Skill:** Understanding and using vocabulary; recognizing sentence structure.

NAME _____

BEGINNING SOUND S

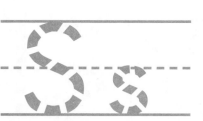  

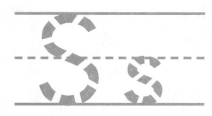  

35

Directions: Have your child trace Ss at the beginning of each row. Ask your child to name the pictures, then circle those with the beginning sound s. ***Skill:*** Identifying the beginning sound s; writing Ss.

COMPREHENSION

See see

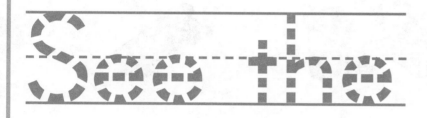

See the  !

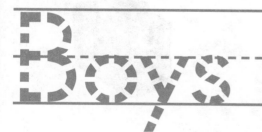 

Boys see!

Directions: Have your child identify the word at the top of the page, then trace and write the words and sentences. Point out the use of capital letters and exclamation points in the sentences.
Skill: Understanding and using vocabulary; recognizing sentence structure.

BEGINNING SOUND P

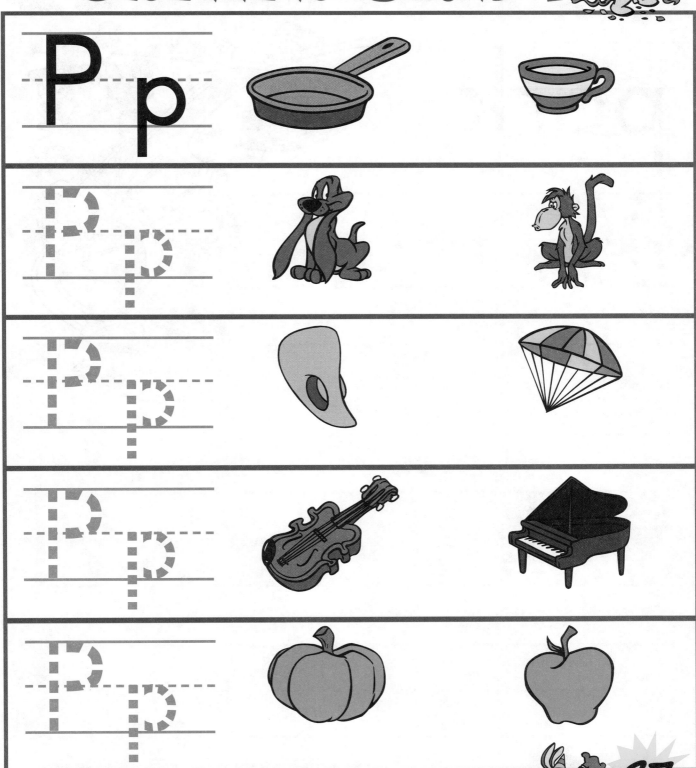

Directions: Have your child trace Pp at the beginning of each row. Ask your child to name the pictures, then circle those with the beginning sound p. **Skill:** Identifying the beginning sound p; writing Pp.

COMPREHENSION

park

the park

See the park!

38

Directions: Have your child identify the word at the top of the page, then trace and write the words and sentences. Point out the use of capital letters and exclamation points in the sentences.
Skill: Understanding and using vocabulary; recognizing sentence structure.

VOWELS: SHORT U

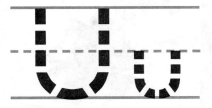   cup

39

COMPREHENSION

The man __.
rides   boys

Jump __!
park   now

See the __.
park   fish

Now the boys __.
jump   see

Directions: Have your child look at the pictures in each box, then circle the word that completes the sentence and describes the picture. **Skill:** Understanding and using vocabulary; recognizing sentence structure.

MATCHING

41

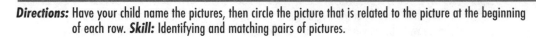
Directions: Have your child name the pictures, then circle the picture that is related to the picture at the beginning of each row. **Skill:** Identifying and matching pairs of pictures.

BEGINNING SOUND C

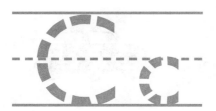  

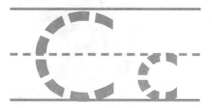  

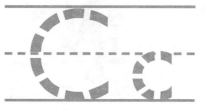  

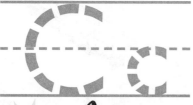  

Directions: Have your child trace Cc at the beginning of each row. Ask your child to name the pictures, then circle those with the beginning sound c. **Skill:** Identifying the beginning sound c; writing Cc.

COMPREHENSION

Can can

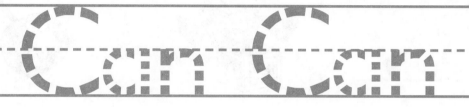

Can Can

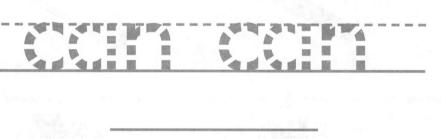

can can

_____

- - - - - - - - - - -

_____ the man fish?

_____

- - - - - - - - - - -

The man _____ fish.

Directions: Have your child identify the word at the top of the page. Ask your child to trace and write the words, then place them in the sentences at the bottom of the page. Point out the use of capital letters, the question mark and the period in the sentences. **Skill:** Understanding and using vocabulary; recognizing sentence structure.

BEGINNING SOUND Y

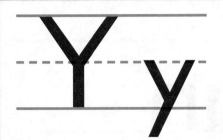  

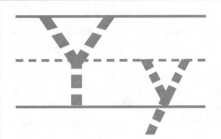  

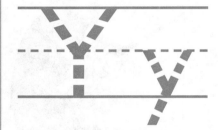  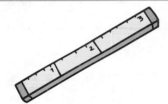

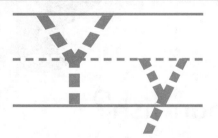  

 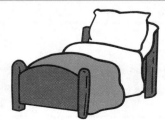 

44

Directions: Have your child trace Yy at the beginning of each row. Ask your child to name the pictures, then circle those with the beginning sound y. ***Skill:*** Identifying the beginning sound y; writing Yy.

You you

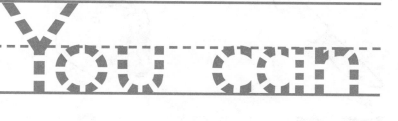

You can  .

 .

Can you 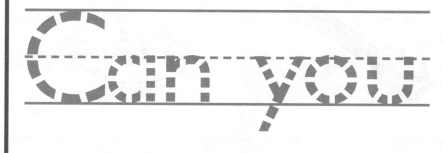  ?

  ?

Directions: Have your child identify the word at the top of the page, then trace and write the words and sentences. Point out the use of capital letters, periods and question marks in the sentences.
Skill: Understanding and using vocabulary; recognizing sentence structure.

BEGINNING SOUND T

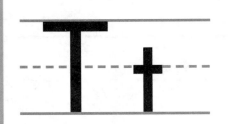

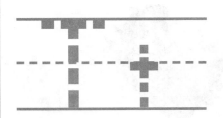

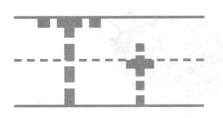

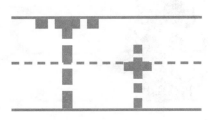

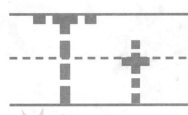

Directions: Have your child trace Tt at the beginning of each row. Ask your child to name the pictures, then circle those with the beginning sound t. **Skill:** Identifying the beginning sound t; writing Tt.

COMPREHENSION

to

to   to   to

jump to the

Directions: Have your child identify the word at the top of the page, then trace and write the words and sentences. Point out the use of capital letters and periods in the sentences. **Skill:** Understanding and using vocabulary; recognizing sentence structure.

BEGINNING SOUND W

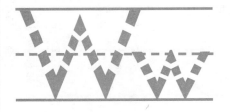

Directions: Have your child trace Ww at the beginning of each row. Ask your child to name the pictures, then circle those with the beginning sound w. **Skill:** Identifying the beginning sound w; writing Ww.

BEGINNING SOUND Z

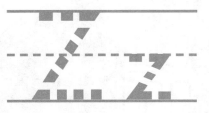  

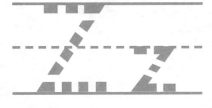  

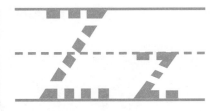  

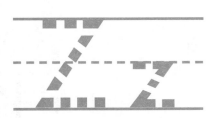

49

Directions: Have your child trace Zz at the beginning of each row. Ask your child to name the pictures, then circle those with the beginning sound z. **Skill:** Identifying the beginning sound z; writing Zz.

COMPREHENSION

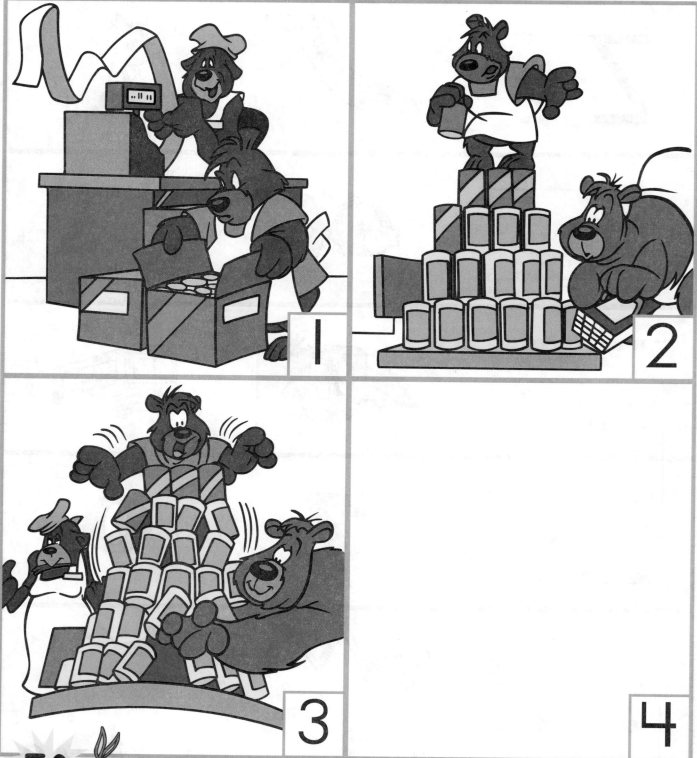

50

Directions: Have your child identify the pictures in each box and explain the sequence of events. Ask your child to draw a picture in the last box to show what happens next. **Skill:** Identifying a sequence of events; predicting an outcome.

VOWELS: SHORT I

I i   d**i**g

Directions: Have your child trace Ii at the beginning of each row. Ask your child to say the word *dig* while listening for the short i sound. Have your child name the pictures, then circle those that have the same short i sound as the picture at the top of the page. **Skill:** Identifying the short i vowel sound; writing Ii.

COMPREHENSION

The man rides __ a park.

to   and

The man __ jump.

see   can

Can __ jump?

you   and

__ you see?

To   Can

Directions: Have your child identify the pictures in each box, then circle the word that completes the sentence and describes the picture. **Skill:** Understanding and using vocabulary; recognizing sentence structure.

BEGINNING SOUND L

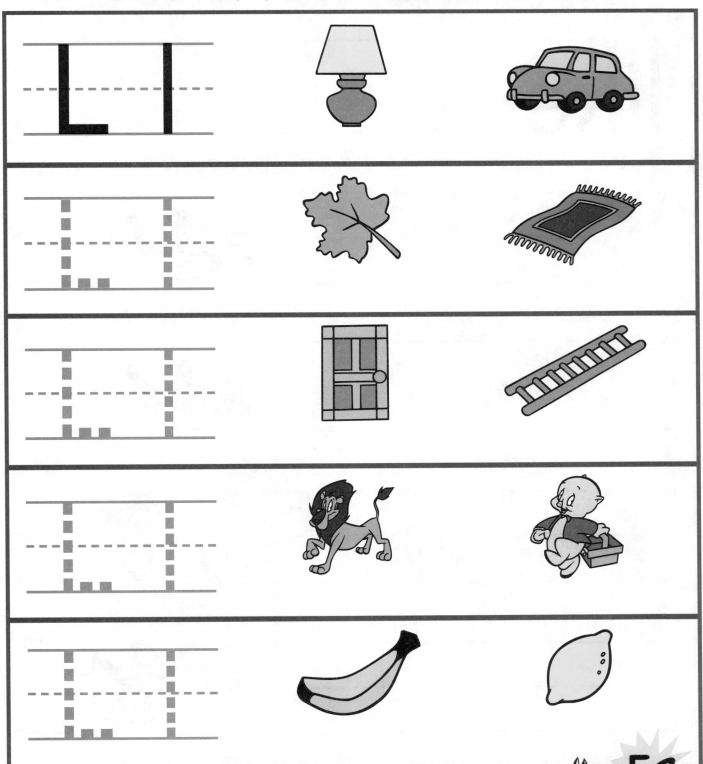

53

Directions: Have your child trace Ll at the beginning of each row. Ask your child to name the pictures, then circle those with the beginning sound l. **Skill:** Identifying the beginning sound l; writing Ll.

COMPREHENSION

like

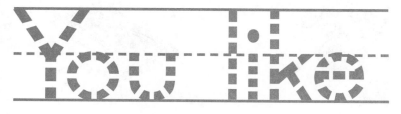

Directions: Have your child identify the word at the top of the page, then trace and write the words and sentences. Point out the use of capital letters and periods in the sentences. **Skill:** Understanding and using vocabulary; recognizing sentence structure.

BEGINNING SOUND D

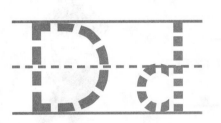

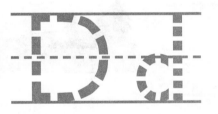

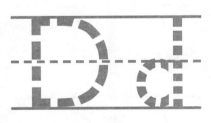

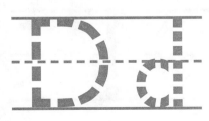

55

Directions: Have your child trace Dd at the beginning of each row. Ask your child to name the pictures, then circle those with the beginning sound d. **Skill:** Identifying the beginning sound d; writing Dd.

COMPREHENSION

down

down down

Jump down!

Directions: Have your child identify the word at the top of the page, then trace and write the words and sentences. Point out the use of capital letters and exclamation points in the sentences.
Skill: Understanding and using vocabulary; recognizing sentence structure.

BEGINNING SOUND V

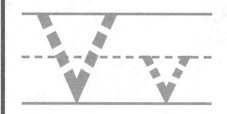  

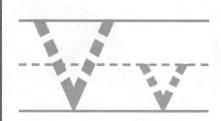  

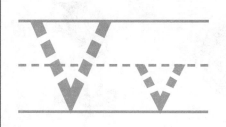  

Directions: Have your child trace Vv at the beginning of each row. Ask your child to name the pictures, then circle those with the beginning sound v. **Skill:** Identifying the beginning sound v; writing Vv.

NAME

BEGINNING SOUND QU

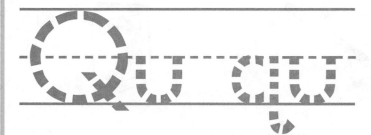  

58

Directions: Have your child trace Qu/qu at the beginning of each row. Ask your child to name the pictures, then circle those with the beginning sound qu. **Skill:** Identifying the beginning sound qu; writing Qu/qu.

FINAL SOUND X

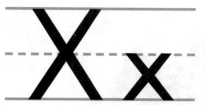  

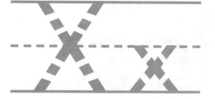

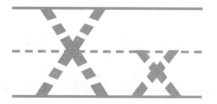  

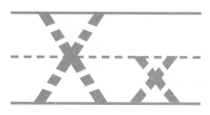  

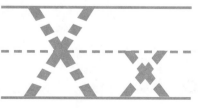  

Directions: Have your child trace Xx at the beginning of each row. Ask your child to name the pictures, then circle those with the final sound x. *Skill:* Identifying the final sound x; writing Xx.

COMPREHENSION

Aa

A man rides.

A man rides to a park.

_____ man rides to _____ park.

 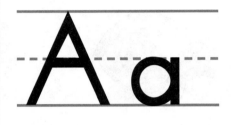

Directions: Have your child identify the word at the top of the page, then trace and write the sentences and words. Point out the use of capital letters and periods in the sentences. **Skill:** Understanding and using vocabulary; recognizing sentence structure.

COMPREHENSION

up

up up

Girls jump up!

Directions: Have your child identify the word at the top of the page, then trace and write the words and sentences. Point out the use of capital letters and exclamation points in the sentences.
Skill: Understanding and using vocabulary; recognizing sentence structure.

ALPHABETICAL ORDER

Directions: Have your child connect the dots in alphabetical order from A to Z to form a picture. **Skill:** Recognizing alphabetical order.

NAME _____

VOWELS: SHORT O

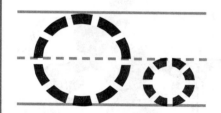  

top

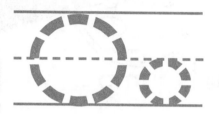   

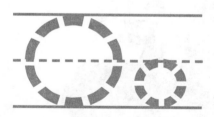   

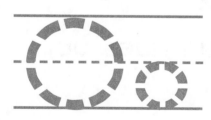   

Directions: Have your child trace Oo at the beginning of each row. Ask your child to say the word *top* while listening for the short o sound. Have your child name the pictures, then circle those that have the same short o sound as the picture at the top of the page. **Skill:** Identifying the short o vowel sound; writing Oo.

63

NAME _____

The man rides ___.

up   down

The girls jump ___.

down   up

Girls ___ a park.

fish   like

___ man rides up.

See   A

64

ANSWER KEY

Top, Bottom

Directions: Have your child look at the pictures, then circle the picture in each row that shows top and put an X on the picture that shows bottom. **Skill:** Identifying the positions top and bottom.

3

Left, Right

4

Directions: Have your child look at the picture, then color the ball on the left green, color the ball on the right red, then circle the characters on the left. **Skill:** Identifying the positions left and right.

Matching

s	s	e	s	w
i	l	i	i	y
p	p	d	b	p
b	b	c	b	d
G	D	G	Q	G
N	N	R	N	M
Y	J	Y	P	Y
J	J	P	J	I

Directions: Have your child look at the letter in the box at the beginning of each row, then circle the two letters in each row that are the same. **Skill:** Matching capital and lowercase letters.

5

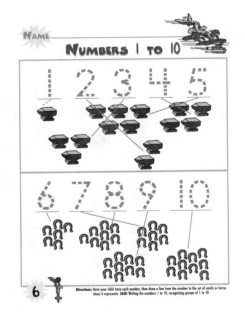

Numbers 1 to 10

1 2 3 4 5

6 7 8 9 10

6

Directions: Have your child trace each number, then draw a line from the number to the set of anvils or horseshoes it represents. **Skill:** Writing the numbers 1 to 10; recognizing groups of 1 to 10.

Beginning Sound K

Kk	key	house
Kk	horse	king
Kk	kitten	wagon
Kk	lion	kangaroo
Kk	tricycle	kite

Directions: Have your child trace Kk at the beginning of each row. Ask your child to name the pictures, then circle those with the beginning sound k. **Skill:** Identifying the beginning sound k; writing Kk.

7

Comprehension

The the

the

the

The

The

8

Directions: Have your child identify the word at the top of the page, then trace and write the words and sentences. Point out the use of capital letters and periods in the sentences. **Skill:** Understanding and using vocabulary; recognizing sentence structure.

Answer Key

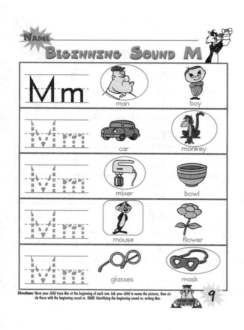

Name

Beginning Sound M

Mm	man	boy
Mm	car	monkey
Mm	mixer	bowl
Mm	mouse	flower
Mm	glasses	mask

Directions: Have your child trace Mm at the beginning of each row. Ask your child to name the pictures, then circle those with the beginning sound m. **Skill:** Identifying the beginning sound m; writing Mm.

9

Name

Comprehension

The the man

the

the

The man

The man

10

Directions: Have your child identify the words at the top of the page, then trace and write the words and sentences. Point out the use of capital letters and periods in the sentences. **Skill:** Understanding and using vocabulary; recognizing sentence structure.

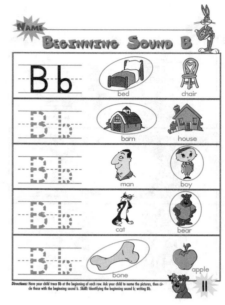

Name

Beginning Sound B

B b	bed	chair
B b	barn	house
B b	man	boy
B b	cat	bear
B b	bone	apple

Directions: Have your child trace Bb at the beginning of each row. Ask your child to name the pictures, then circle those with the beginning sound b. **Skill:** Identifying the beginning sound b; writing Bb.

11

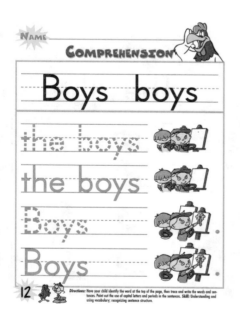

Name

Comprehension

Boys boys

the boys

the boys

Boys

Boys

12

Directions: Have your child identify the word at the top of the page, then trace and write the words and sentences. Point out the use of capital letters and periods in the sentences. **Skill:** Understanding and using vocabulary; recognizing sentence structure.

Name

Sequence

Directions: Have your child identify the scenes in each box, then ask your child to number the pictures in the order in which they take place. **Skill:** Identifying a sequence of events.

13

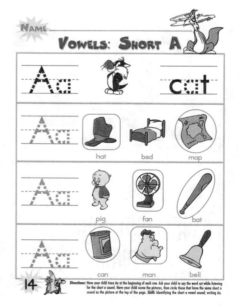

Name

Vowels: Short A

Aa		cat
Aa	hat	bed	map
Aa	pig	fan	bat
Aa	can	man	bell

14

Directions: Have your child trace Aa at the beginning of each row. Ask your child to say the word while listening for the short a sound. Have your child name the pictures, then circle those that have the same short a sound as the picture at the top of the page. **Skill:** Identifying the short a vowel sound; writing Aa.

66

ANSWER KEY

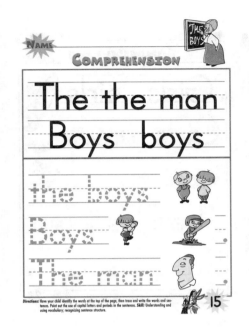

COMPREHENSION

The the man
Boys boys

the boys

Boys

The man

Directions: Have your child identify the words at the top of the page, then trace and write the words and sentences. Point out the use of capital letters and periods in the sentences. Skill: Understanding and using vocabulary; recognizing sentence structure.

15

CLASSIFYING

Sylvester | Claude
Pussyfoot | Hector

chair | banana
bench | sofa

ball | game
horse | book

doll | sandwich
merry-go-round | tricycle

16

Directions: Have your child identify the pictures, then circle those in each box that belong in the same category: the cat family, things to sit on, things to play with and things to ride. Skill: Identifying and classifying objects.

FIRST, MIDDLE, LAST

Directions: Have your child identify the pictures, then circle the last character in the first row, the middle character in the second row, the first train in the third row and the middle character in the fourth row. Skill: Identifying the positions first, middle and last.

17

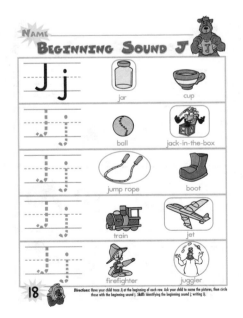

BEGINNING SOUND J

J j | jar | cup
J | ball | jack-in-the-box
J | jump rope | boot
J | train | jet
J | firefighter | juggler

18

Directions: Have your child trace Jj at the beginning of each row. Ask your child to name the pictures, then circle those with the beginning sound j. Skill: Identifying the beginning sound j; writing Jj.

COMPREHENSION

Jump jump

The boys jump

The boys jump.

Jump boys!

Jump boys!

Directions: Have your child identify the word at the top of the page, then trace and write the words and sentences. Point out the use of capital letters, periods and exclamation points in the sentences. Skill: Understanding and using vocabulary; recognizing sentence structure.

19

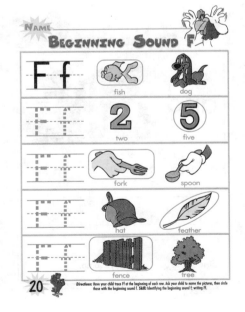

BEGINNING SOUND F

F f | fish | dog
F | two | five
F | fork | spoon
F | hat | feather
F | fence | tree

20

Directions: Have your child trace Ff at the beginning of each row. Ask your child to name the pictures, then circle those with the beginning sound f. Skill: Identifying the beginning sound f; writing Ff.

ANSWER KEY

COMPREHENSION

fish

Boys fish.

Boys fish.

The boys fish.

The boys fish.

Directions: Have your child identify the word at the top of the page, then trace and write the words and sentences. Point out the use of capital letters and periods in the sentences. **Skill:** Understanding and using vocabulary; recognizing sentence structure.

21

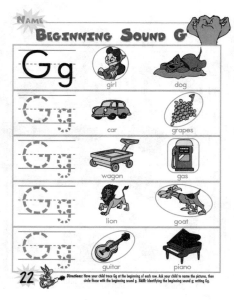

BEGINNING SOUND G

G g	girl	dog
G g	car	grapes
G g	wagon	gas
G g	lion	goat
G g	guitar	piano

22 *Directions:* Have your child trace Gg at the beginning of each row. Ask your child to name the pictures, then circle those with the beginning sound g. **Skill:** Identifying the beginning sound g; writing Gg.

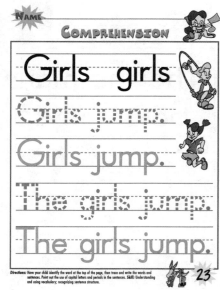

COMPREHENSION

Girls girls

Girls jump.

Girls jump.

The girls jump.

The girls jump.

Directions: Have your child identify the word at the top of the page, then trace and write the words and sentences. Point out the use of capital letters and periods in the sentences. **Skill:** Understanding and using vocabulary; recognizing sentence structure.

23

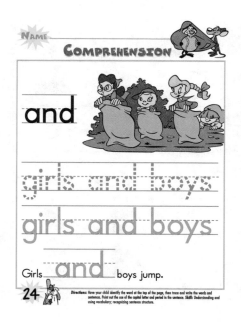

COMPREHENSION

and

girls and boys

girls and boys

and

Girls _____ boys jump.

24 *Directions:* Have your child identify the word at the top of the page, then trace and write the words and sentences. Point out the use of the capital letter and period in the sentence. **Skill:** Understanding and using vocabulary; recognizing sentence structure.

SEQUENCE

4	2
3	1
2	1
3	4

Directions: Ask your child to identify the pictures in each group, then number the pictures in the order in which they take place. **Skill:** Identifying a sequence of events.

25

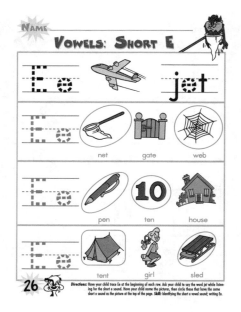

VOWELS: SHORT E

E e		jet
E e	net	gate	web
E e	pen	ten	house
E e	tent	girl	sled

26 *Directions:* Have your child trace Ee at the beginning of each row. Ask your child to say the word jet while listening for the short e sound. Have your child name the pictures, then circle those that have the same short e sound as the picture at the top of the page. **Skill:** Identifying the short e vowel sound; writing Ee.

ANSWER KEY

COMPREHENSION

Girls _ boys fish.
(and) the

Boys and _ jump.
fish (girls)

_ girls!
Boys (Jump)

The girls _.
(fish) jump

Directions: Have your child look at the pictures in each box, then circle the word that completes the sentence and describes the picture. **Skill:** Understanding and using vocabulary; recognizing sentence structure.

27

CLASSIFYING

horse — horseshoe — Nero — Claude

anvil — skis — Pussyfoot — Pepe

traffic officer — firefighter — carrot — turnip

taxi driver — farmer — celery — candy bar

Directions: Have your child identify the pictures, then circle those in each box that belong in the same category: things a cowboy uses, the cat family, people who work in the city, and things that grow. **Skill:** Identifying and classifying objects.

28

SEQUENCE

1 | 3

4 | 2

1 | 2

4 | 3

Directions: Have your child identify the scenes in each box, then ask your child to number the pictures in the order in which they take place. **Skill:** Identifying a sequence of events.

29

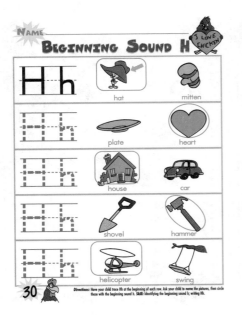

BEGINNING SOUND H

I LOVE CHICKEN

Hh — hat / mitten

Hh — plate / heart

Hh — house / car

Hh — shovel / hammer

Hh — helicopter / swing

Directions: Have your child trace Hh at the beginning of each row. Ask your child to name the pictures, then circle those with the beginning sound h. **Skill:** Identifying the beginning sound h; writing Hh.

30

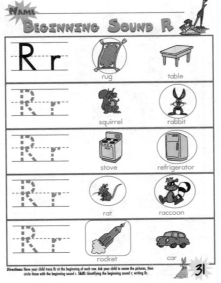

BEGINNING SOUND R

Rr — rug / table

Rr — squirrel / rabbit

Rr — stove / refrigerator

Rr — rat / raccoon

Rr — rocket / car

Directions: Have your child trace Rr at the beginning of each row. Ask your child to name the pictures, then circle those with the beginning sound r. **Skill:** Identifying the beginning sound r; writing Rr.

31

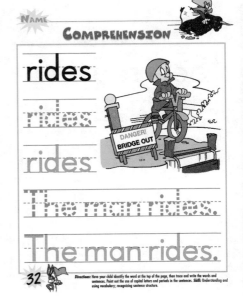

COMPREHENSION

rides

rides

rides

The man rides.

The man rides.

DANGER! BRIDGE OUT

Directions: Have your child identify the word at the top of the page, then trace and write the words and sentences. Point out the use of capital letters and periods in the sentences. **Skill:** Understanding and using vocabulary; recognizing sentence structure.

32

ANSWER KEY

NAME _____
BEGINNING SOUND N

Nn	9 nine	peanut
Nn	ear	neck
Nn	cage	nest
Nn	nickel	shell
Nn	newspaper	camera

Directions: Have your child trace Nn at the beginning of each row. Ask your child to name the pictures, then circle those with the beginning sound n. *Skill:* Identifying the beginning sound n; writing Nn. **33**

NAME _____
COMPREHENSION

Now now

Jump now.

Jump now.

Now jump.

Now jump.

34 *Directions:* Have your child identify the word at the top of the page, then trace and write the words and sentences. Point out the use of capital letters and periods in the sentences. *Skill:* Understanding and using vocabulary; recognizing sentence structure.

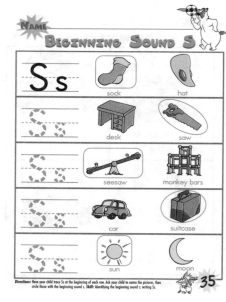

NAME _____
BEGINNING SOUND S

Ss	sock	hat
Ss	desk	saw
Ss	seesaw	monkey bars
Ss	car	suitcase
Ss	sun	moon

Directions: Have your child trace Ss at the beginning of each row. Ask your child to name the pictures, then circle those with the beginning sound s. *Skill:* Identifying the beginning sound s; writing Ss. **35**

NAME _____
COMPREHENSION

See see

See the [ ] !

See the [ ] !

Boys see !

Boys see !

36 *Directions:* Have your child identify the word at the top of the page, then trace and write the words and sentences. *Skill:* Understanding and using vocabulary; recognizing sentence structure.

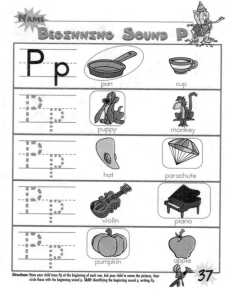

NAME _____
BEGINNING SOUND P

Pp	pan	cup
Pp	puppy	monkey
Pp	hat	parachute
Pp	violin	piano
Pp	pumpkin	apple

Directions: Have your child trace Pp at the beginning of each row. Ask your child to name the pictures, then circle those with the beginning sound p. *Skill:* Identifying the beginning sound p; writing Pp. **37**

NAME _____
COMPREHENSION

park

the park

the park

See the park!

See the park!

38 *Directions:* Have your child identify the word at the top of the page, then trace and write the words and sentences. Point out the use of capital letters and exclamation points in the sentences. *Skill:* Understanding and using vocabulary; recognizing sentence structure.

ANSWER KEY

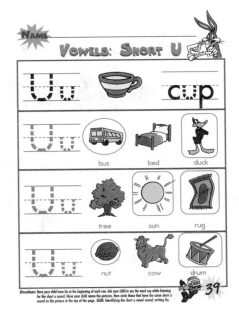

VOWELS: SHORT U

Uu	[cup]	cup

Uu	bus	bed	duck

Uu	tree	sun	rug

Uu	nut	cow	drum

Directions: Have your child trace Uu at the beginning of each row. Ask your child to say the word cup while listening for the short u sound. Have your child name the pictures, then circle those that have the same short u sound as the picture at the top of the page. **Skill:** Identifying the short u vowel sound; writing Uu.

39

COMPREHENSION

The man ___. (rides) boys	Jump ___! park (now)
See the ___. (park) fish	Now the boys ___. jump (see)

40

Directions: Have your child look at the pictures in each box, then circle the word that completes the sentence and describes the picture. **Skill:** Understanding and using vocabulary; recognizing sentence structure.

MATCHING

paintbrush	apple	doll	paint
cup	book	saucer	car
toothbrush	teeth	snow figure	bicycle
watering can	comb	plant	monkey
saw	hat	whistle	board

Directions: Have your child name the pictures, then circle the picture that is related to the picture at the beginning of each row. **Skill:** Identifying and matching pairs of pictures.

41

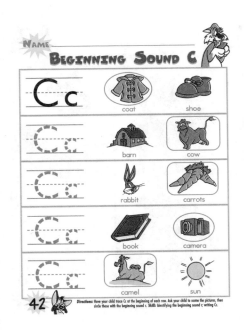

BEGINNING SOUND C

Cc	coat	shoe
Cc	barn	cow
Cc	rabbit	carrots
Cc	book	camera
Cc	camel	sun

42

Directions: Have your child trace Cc at the beginning of each row. Ask your child to name the pictures, then circle those with the beginning sound c. **Skill:** Identifying the beginning sound c; writing Cc.

COMPREHENSION

Can can

Can Can

can can

Can the man fish?

The man can fish.

43

Directions: Have your child identify the word at the top of the page. Ask your child to trace and write the words, then place them in the sentences at the bottom of the page. Point out the use of capital letters, the question mark and the period in the sentences. **Skill:** Understanding and using vocabulary; recognizing sentence structure.

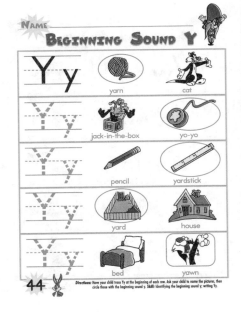

BEGINNING SOUND Y

Yy	yarn	cat
Yy	jack-in-the-box	yo-yo
Yy	pencil	yardstick
Yy	yard	house
Yy	bed	yawn

44

Directions: Have your child trace Yy at the beginning of each row. Ask your child to name the pictures, then circle those with the beginning sound y. **Skill:** Identifying the beginning sound y; writing Yy.

Answer Key

Comprehension

You you
You can [.]
You can [.]
Can you [?]
Can you [?]

Directions: Have your child identify the word at the top of the page, then trace and write the words and sentences. Point out the use of capital letters, periods and question marks in the sentences. *Skill:* Understanding and using vocabulary; recognizing sentence structure.

45

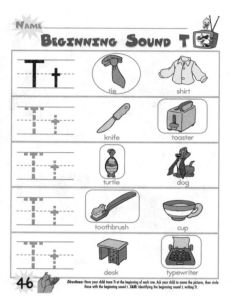

Beginning Sound T

T t — tie, shirt
T t — knife, toaster
T t — turtle, dog
T t — toothbrush, cup
T t — desk, typewriter

46

Directions: Have your child trace Tt at the beginning of each row. Ask your child to name the pictures, then circle those with the beginning sound t. *Skill:* Identifying the beginning sound t; writing Tt.

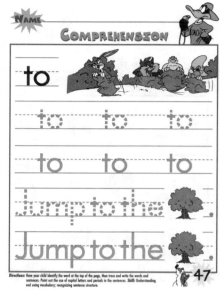

Comprehension

to
to   to   to
to   to   to
Jump to the
Jump to the [.]

47

Directions: Have your child identify the word at the top of the page, then trace and write the words and sentences. Point out the use of capital letters and periods in the sentences. *Skill:* Understanding and using vocabulary; recognizing sentence structure.

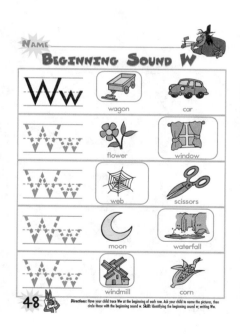

Beginning Sound W

W w — wagon, car
W — flower, window
W — web, scissors
W — moon, waterfall
W — windmill, corn

48

Directions: Have your child trace Ww at the beginning of each row. Ask your child to name the pictures, then circle those with the beginning sound w. *Skill:* Identifying the beginning sound w; writing Ww.

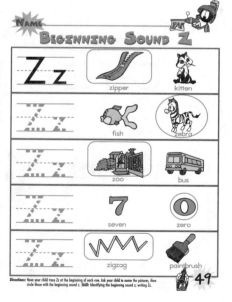

Beginning Sound Z

Z z — zipper, kitten
Z z — fish, zebra
Z z — zoo, bus
Z z — seven, zero
Z z — zigzag, paintbrush

Directions: Have your child trace Zz at the beginning of each row. Ask your child to name the pictures, then circle those with the beginning sound z. *Skill:* Identifying the beginning sound z; writing Zz.

49

Comprehension

1   2
3   Answers will vary.   4

50

Directions: Have your child identify the pictures in each box and explain the sequence of events. Ask your child to draw a picture in the last box to show what happens next. *Skill:* Identifying a sequence of events; predicting an outcome.

72

Answer Key

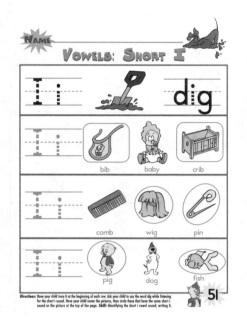

Vowels: Short I

I i   dig

I i — bib   baby   crib

I i — comb   wig   pin

I i — pig   dog   fish

51

Comprehension

The man rides ___ a park.   (to)   and

The man ___ jump.   see   (can)

Can ___ jump?   (you)   and

___ you see?   To   (Can)

52

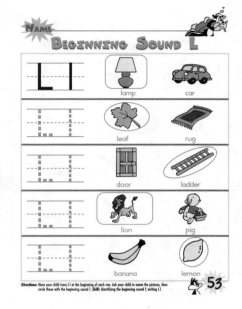

Beginning Sound L

L l   lamp   car

L l — leaf   rug

L l — door   ladder

L l — lion   pig

L l — banana   lemon

53

Comprehension

like

You like

You like

You like to

You like to .

54

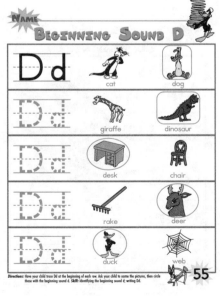

Beginning Sound D

D d   cat   dog

D d — giraffe   dinosaur

D d — desk   chair

D d — rake   deer

D d — duck   web

55

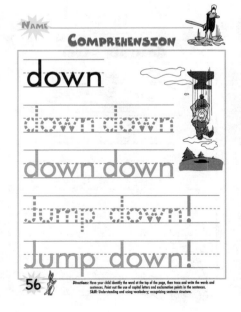

Comprehension

down

down down

down down

Jump down!

Jump down!

56

ANSWER KEY

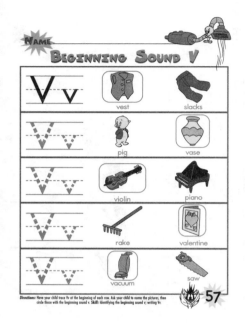

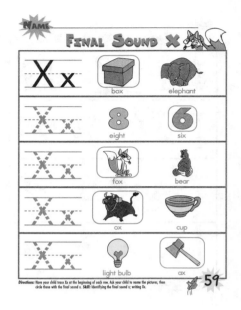

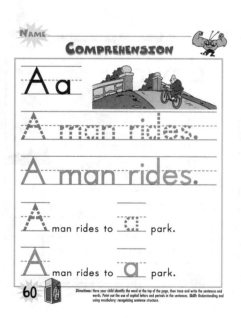

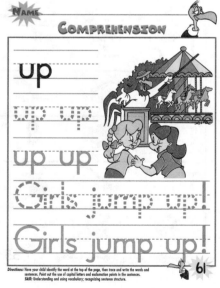

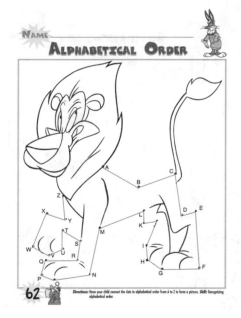

ANSWER KEY

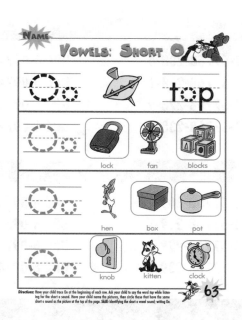

Look for all of these entertaining and educational titles in

The McGraw-Hill Junior Academic™ Workbook Series

Toddler

My Colors Go 'Round	ISBN 1-57768-208-4	UPC 6-09746-45118-5
My 1, 2, 3's	ISBN 1-57768-218-1	UPC 6-09746-45128-4
My A, B, C's	ISBN 1-57768-228-9	UPC 6-09746-45138-3
My Ups and Downs	ISBN 1-57768-238-6	UPC 6-09746-45148-2

Preschool

MATH	ISBN 1-57768-209-2	UPC 6-09746-45119-2
READING	ISBN 1-57768-219-X	UPC 6-09746-45129-1
VOWEL SOUNDS	ISBN 1-57768-229-7	UPC 6-09746-45139-0
SOUND PATTERNS	ISBN 1-57768-239-4	UPC 6-09746-45149-9

Kindergarten

MATH	ISBN 1-57768-200-9	UPC 6-09746-45110-9
READING	ISBN 1-57768-210-6	UPC 6-09746-45120-8
PHONICS	ISBN 1-57768-220-3	UPC 6-09746-45130-7
THINKING SKILLS	ISBN 1-57768-230-0	UPC 6-09746-45140-6

Grade 1

MATH	ISBN 1-57768-201-7	UPC 6-09746-45111-6
READING	ISBN 1-57768-211-4	UPC 6-09746-45121-5
PHONICS	ISBN 1-57768-221-1	UPC 6-09746-45131-4
WORD BUILDERS	ISBN 1-57768-231-9	UPC 6-09746-45141-3

Grade 2

MATH	ISBN 1-57768-202-5	UPC 6-09746-45112-3
READING	ISBN 1-57768-212-2	UPC 6-09746-45122-2
PHONICS	ISBN 1-57768-222-X	UPC 6-09746-45132-1
WORD BUILDERS	ISBN 1-57768-232-7	UPC 6-09746-45142-0

It's Serious Fun!!

Offers a selection of workbooks to meet all your needs.

Look for all of these fine educational workbooks
in the McGraw-Hill Learning Materials SPECTRUM Series.
All workbooks meet school curriculum guidelines and correspond to
The McGraw-Hill Companies classroom textbooks.

SPECTRUM SERIES

GEOGRAPHY

Full-color, three-part lessons strengthen geography knowledge and map reading skills. Focusing on five geographic themes including location, place, human/environmental interaction, movement, and regions. Over 150 pages. Glossary of geographical terms and answer key included.

TITLE	ISBN	PRICE
Grade 3, Communities	1-57768-153-3	$7.95
Grade 4, Regions	1-57768-154-1	$7.95
Grade 5, USA	1-57768-155-X	$7.95
Grade 6, World	1-57768-156-8	$7.95

MATH

Features easy-to-follow instructions that give students a clear path to success. This series has comprehensive coverage of the basic skills, helping children to master math fundamentals. Over 150 pages. Answer key included.

TITLE	ISBN	PRICE
Grade 1	1-57768-111-8	$6.95
Grade 2	1-57768-112-6	$6.95
Grade 3	1-57768-113-4	$6.95
Grade 4	1-57768-114-2	$6.95
Grade 5	1-57768-115-0	$6.95
Grade 6	1-57768-116-9	$6.95
Grade 7	1-57768-117-7	$6.95
Grade 8	1-57768-118-5	$6.95

PHONICS

Provides everything children need to build multiple skills in language. Focusing on phonics, structural analysis, and dictionary skills, this series also offers creative ideas for using phonics and word study skills in other language arts. Over 200 pages. Answer key included.

TITLE	ISBN	PRICE
Grade K	1-57768-120-7	$6.95
Grade 1	1-57768-121-5	$6.95
Grade 2	1-57768-122-3	$6.95
Grade 3	1-57768-123-1	$6.95
Grade 4	1-57768-124-X	$6.95
Grade 5	1-57768-125-8	$6.95
Grade 6	1-57768-126-6	$6.95

READING

This full-color series creates an enjoyable reading environment, even for below-average readers. Each book contains captivating content, colorful characters, and compelling illustrations, so children are eager to find out what happens next. Over 150 pages. Answer key included.

TITLE	ISBN	PRICE
Grade K	1-57768-130-4	$6.95
Grade 1	1-57768-131-2	$6.95
Grade 2	1-57768-132-0	$6.95
Grade 3	1-57768-133-9	$6.95
Grade 4	1-57768-134-7	$6.95
Grade 5	1-57768-135-5	$6.95
Grade 6	1-57768-136-3	$6.95

SPELLING

This full-color series links spelling to reading and writing and increases skills in words and meanings, consonant and vowel spellings, and proofreading practice. Over 200 pages. Speller dictionary and answer key included.

TITLE	ISBN	PRICE
Grade 1	1-57768-161-4	$7.95
Grade 2	1-57768-162-2	$7.95
Grade 3	1-57768-163-0	$7.95
Grade 4	1-57768-164-9	$7.95
Grade 5	1-57768-165-7	$7.95
Grade 6	1-57768-166-5	$7.95

WRITING

Lessons focus on creative and expository writing using clearly stated objectives and pre-writing exercises. Eight essential reading skills are applied. Activities include main idea, sequence, comparison, detail, fact and opinion, cause and effect, and making a point. Over 130 pages. Answer key included.

TITLE	ISBN	PRICE
Grade 1	1-57768-141-X	$6.95
Grade 2	1-57768-142-8	$6.95
Grade 3	1-57768-143-6	$6.95
Grade 4	1-57768-144-4	$6.95
Grade 5	1-57768-145-2	$6.95
Grade 6	1-57768-146-0	$6.95
Grade 7	1-57768-147-9	$6.95
Grade 8	1-57768-148-7	$6.95

TEST PREP from the Nation's #1 Testing Company

Prepares children to do their best on current editions of the five major standardized tests. Activities reinforce test-taking skills through examples, tips, practice, and timed exercises. Subjects include reading, math, and language. Over 150 pages. Answer key included.

TITLE	ISBN	PRICE
Grade 3	1-57768-103-7	$8.95
Grade 4	1-57768-104-5	$8.95
Grade 5	1-57768-105-3	$8.95
Grade 6	1-57768-106-1	$8.95
Grade 7	1-57768-107-X	$8.95
Grade 8	1-57768-108-8	$8.95